ROBERT BURTON

ANIMAL HOMES

ARCTIC

photographs by Oxford Scientific Films

 Belitha Press

First published in Great Britain in 1991 by
Belitha Press Limited
31 Newington Green, London N16 9PU
Text copyright © Robert Burton 1991
Photographs copyright © Oxford Scientific
Films and individual copyright holders 1991
Printed in Singapore for Imago Publishing

ISBN 1 85561 042 6

British Library Cataloguing in Publication Data
CIP data for this book is available from the British Library

The publishers wish to thank the following for permission
to reproduce copyright material:

Oxford Scientific Films and individual copyright
holders on the following pages: Tony Allen 8, 9, Robert
Burton 4, Animals Animals/E. R. Degginger 18, Animals
Animals/David C. Fritts 2, Frank Huber 3, Animals
Animals/Kevin Jackson 20, Animals Animals/Richard
Kolar 16, Animals Animals/J. and C. Kroeger 19, Lon E.
Lauber 12, T. S. McCann 23, back cover, Tony Martin 6,
Animals Animals/Brian Milne 7, 11, 13, Owen Newman
17, Carsten R. Oleson 10, 21, Partridge Productions 14,
Tom Uhlrich front cover, 5, 15, 22

The Arctic is a cold place. In winter it is very cold, colder than the inside of a deep freeze. Everywhere is covered with snow and ice. It stays dark all winter because the sun sets and then doesn't come up again for many weeks. The summer is much more pleasant. The sun shines all the time and the snow melts. For a few weeks there are plenty of plants and insects for the animals to eat. It is never warm enough in the Arctic **tundra** for trees to grow.

Caribou, which are also called reindeer, are deer that live in **herds**. They find food in winter by digging holes in the snow to reach lichens and other plants hidden underneath. Their **calves** are born in spring. By the time winter arrives they will be big enough to follow their parents to new feeding grounds. Some herds travel hundreds of kilometres.

Muskoxen have enormously thick coats. Under the long black hair there is a layer of very fine wool that helps to keep them warm in the coldest winter. When **blizzards** blow, a herd of muskoxen will huddle together for extra shelter.

The main hunters of muskoxen are wolves. When a herd is attacked by wolves, the muskoxen form a line facing them. If a wolf comes too close, one muskox will charge it and try to stab the wolf with its sharp horns. If the wolves try to get behind them some muskoxen will turn to face them again so there are always sharp horns facing the wolves. The muskox calves stay safe from the wolves by keeping close to their parents.

The Arctic hare's family of eight **leverets** are born in a hollow in the ground called a **form**. When they are only a few days old the mother hare goes off and leaves them to look after themselves. She still comes back once a day to feed the leverets though. After a feed the leverets hop away from the form and spend their time exploring and nibbling plants. When it is feeding time again they return to the form. There they wait for their mother to come back and feed them.

Arctic hares have to stay watchful all the time because they are hunted for food by other animals. Their large eyes and ears help them to see and hear well. They stand on their hind legs to get a better view of their surroundings. At the first sign of danger they run away at high speed.

When the snow melts in spring the **tundra** becomes flooded with water. The pink-footed goose makes a big pile of grass and other plants and lays her eggs in a nest on the top, where they stay dry. The eggs are kept warm by the female goose while her mate, the gander, stands guard. She plucks fluffy feathers from her body to line the nest and help keep the eggs warm. When she leaves the nest to feed, she covers the eggs with the **down** to hide them.

The **goslings** leave the nest when they are a few days old to follow their parents in search of food. The best plants to eat grow around the edges of lakes. If the geese are chased by foxes or wolves they run into the lake and swim to safety. At the end of the summer the family flies away from the Arctic to spend the winter in a warmer country, such as Britain.

Snow buntings are the most common birds in the Arctic. A **flock** flying together look like snowflakes being blown by the wind. They start to nest while there is still some snow on the ground, finding places where the snow has melted on the hillsides. Each pair of snow buntings finds a sheltered hole under some boulders where they make a nest of dried grass. They add a snug lining of feathers that other birds have lost and left lying on the ground.

After the nestlings have hatched from the eggs the parent snow buntings spend most of their time collecting food. It never really gets dark during the warm Arctic summer and they work almost continuously. At this time of year there are swarms of mosquitoes, midges and other insects for the snow buntings to catch and feed to the young birds.

11

Ptarmigan change their feathers three times a year. They are white in winter, brown in summer and grey in autumn. The ptarmigan turn from white to brown as soon as the snow melts in spring. So they are always difficult to see against the ground. This is specially important for the female ptarmigan when she sits on the nest. If a **predator**, such as a fox, approaches, she keeps very still so that she will not be seen. When the chicks hatch, she stays with them and will attack anything that comes too close.

13

The Arctic winter is not a problem for lemmings. They dig tunnels under the snow so that they can continue feeding on plants even when the weather is very bad. When they have finished feeding, they go back to their snug nests of dried grass.

In some years there are so many lemmings that you can see hundreds of them running over the ground. Lemmings are important **prey** for hunting animals such as Arctic foxes,

snowy owls and long-tailed skuas. When there are few
lemmings these animals must travel elsewhere to search for
food or else go hungry.

Long-tailed skuas visit the **tundra** every summer to nest.
They eat anything they can find, such as butterflies and the
eggs and chicks of other birds. But their most important food
is lemmings. If there are not enough lemmings for them to eat
the skuas do not breed.

The snowy owl is a large and fierce hunter of small Arctic animals. Unlike most other Arctic animals it stays white even after the snow has melted. It keeps watch from a **perch** for small animals such as lemmings, goslings or hares. When it spots something the owl flies silently towards the animal and seizes it with its long sharp **talons**.

Prey is carried back to the nest where the young owls wait eagerly. When they are very young the parent tears the food up for them. Later they have to deal with it by themselves. A young snowy owl can swallow a huge lump of meat without choking.

Polar bears spend most of their time hunting seals on the frozen sea of the far north. Sometimes they will wait patiently for a seal to pop up through its breathing hole. They also search for seals lying on the ice and hunt them in the same way that a cat stalks a bird. The bear has to make sure that the seal does not see or smell it, so it creeps up very carefully, then charges at 60 kilometres per hour.

During the winter the female polar bear finds a deep bank of snow. Here she digs a **den** where she will give birth to her **cubs**. The newborn cubs are tiny and weigh only 600-700 grams. (An adult polar bear can weigh up to 300 kilograms – five hundred times heavier.) Their mother keeps them warm by cuddling them until spring. By then they are big enough to follow her when she goes hunting.

In winter the Arctic fox has a thick white coat of fur. This keeps it warm in very cold conditions. Specially furry feet prevent its toes from freezing. Arctic foxes have a hard time in winter because food is hard to find. The birds that they hunt in summer fly away from the Arctic and the lemmings disappear under the snow. Some foxes follow polar bears and eat the left-overs from their meals.

When the snow melts in summer the Arctic fox's white coat turns grey. Its **cubs** are born in a **den** in the middle of summer. When they are old enough, they play outside the den but they will run to safety when their parents' bark warns them of danger.

Seals spend nearly all their lives in the sea. They have to come out of the water to give birth to their pups though. The harp seal comes out onto the ice of the frozen Arctic sea. Its pup is called a whitecoat because of the colour of its fur.

The pup stays with its mother for only ten or twelve days. It grows rapidly until half its weight is a thick layer of fat. This **blubber** will keep the pup warm and nourished until it learns to find its own food.

The walrus is a large seal with long **tusks**. It likes to live where the sea is covered with ice. Walruses use their tusks to pull themselves on to the ice as well as for fighting and feeding. Walruses dive to the seabed and dig in the mud for clams and cockles, which they suck out of their shells.

Index/Glossary